# YOU GUYS

ALSO BY THE AUTHOR

### Poetry
Consciousness
Ardor: Poems of Life
In the Palace of Creation: Selected Works 1969—1999
illustrated by Meagan Shapiro
Changing Woman
Shapes of Self

### Stories
Journeys with Justine, illustrated by Cristina Biaggi
Walk Now in Beauty: The Legend of Changing Woman, illustrated by Ernest Posey

### Essays
Goddesses, Goddesses: Essays by Janine Canan
My Millennium: Culture, Spirituality and the Divine Feminine

### Translations
Under the Azure: Poems of Francis Jammes  (bilingual in German by Peter Geiger)
Star in My Forehead: Selected Poems by Else Lasker-Schüler

### Anthologies
Love Is My Religion, volumes 1, 2, 3, by Mata Amritanandamayi
Garland of Love: 108 Meditations by Mata Amritanandamayi
Messages from Amma: In the Language of the Heart
She Rises like the Sun: Invocations of the Goddess by American Women Poets,
illustrated by Mayumi Oda

# YOU GUYS

## On the Miscondition of Women

## Janine Canan

Regent Press
Berkeley, California
2020

Copyright © 2020 by Janine Canan

paperback
ISBN 13: 978-1-58790-533-9
ISBN 10: 1-58790-533-7

ebook
ISBN 13: 978-1-58790-534-6
ISBN 10: 1-58790-534-5

Library of Congress Cataloging-in-Publication Data

Names: Canan, Janine, author.
Title: You guys : on the miscondition of women / Janine Canan.
Description: First Edition. | Berkeley : Regent Press, 2020. | Summary: "A blood-curdling howl for women to awaken, Janine Canan's poignant and disturbing compendium on the condition of 21st century woman portrays the women we love, hate, pity and are - exposing our tortured relationship to the feminine in an increasingly maled and motherless wasteland of pathological masculinity. Both lamentation and hymn, You Guys is ultimately a tribute to the indomitable potential of Women and the eternal beauty of Life"-- Provided by publisher.
Identifiers: LCCN 2020033959 (print) | LCCN 2020033960 (ebook) | ISBN 9781587905339 (paperback) | ISBN 9781587905346 (kindle edition)
Subjects: LCSH: Women--History--21st century. | Femininity. | Self-esteem.
Classification: LCC HQ1155 .C356 2020 (print) | LCC HQ1155 (ebook) | DDC 305.4209/05--dc23
LC record available at https://lccn.loc.gov/2020033959
LC ebook record available at https://lccn.loc.gov/2020033960

YOU GUYS began in 2008.
The author's work is in the public domain
and may be copied with full credit.

Macufactured in the U.S.A.

REGENT PRESS
Berkeley, California
www.regentpress.net

Dedicated to Mother Earth,
courageous women everywhere
and the men who clear the way....

# CONTENTS

### YOU GUYS / 9
▽

### GIRLS / 17
▽

### SEXEES / 29
▽

### WIVES / 35
▽

### PATRIARCHEES / 45
▽

### WOMAN HATERS / 69

SELF DEFORMERS / 75
▽
MEN-WOMEN / 81
▽
REBELS / 91
▽
OUTSIDERS / 99
▽
SURVIVORS / 109
▽
VICTIMS ALL / 112
▽
VICTORS / 131

# YOU GUYS

who were born
in a woman's body

You Guys
who labor and mother
and feel no solidarity with women.

You cheery Guys
who call your girlfriends
Dude

You blithe Guys
happy to be accepted
into his Lordship's gender

You duped Guys
proud of your new title,
blind to its price


You naive Guys who imagine
if you are called guys
you will be equal


You Guys the United Nations says
at the current rate will take a thousand years
to reach equality


You post-woman Guys
sanctified with boy names
like your brothers


You giddy Guys
thrilled to be granted entry
into man's prestigious club

You drowsy Guys who would never dream
of voting for a woman
because she is a woman


You muddled Guys
who actually say voting for a man
is a sign of progress


You post-feminist Guys
allergic to concepts
of woman, feminine and mother.


You cool Guys bored by the hags
who once riled teachers, fathers, husbands,
police, pimps and priests


You co-opted Guys
loyal to patriarchy,
who dishonor your foremothers

You gypped Guys
spawned in a backlash
that turned mainstream, then tidal


You come-lately Guys
who never knew the braves
who confronted misogyny and incinerated it


You entitled Guys who scorn the crones
who rolled away the boulders
and broke down the doors you sweep through


You care-free Guys
thankless to the ladies who liberated you
from kitchen, girdle and high heels.


You unconscious Guys who still don't mind
doing most of the world's work
and owning almost nothing

You long exploited Guys
who do eighty percent of the world's work
and are paid a fraction of man's wage


You impoverished Guys
whose sex makes up
seventy percent of the world's poor


You surcharged Guys
who pay more for healthcare and clothes
than men do


You endangered Guys,
battered and raped
and threatened every day


You exhausted Guys
who have no time to think
about your condition

You gullible Guys
who swallow Male News
uncomplaining


You wired Guys
permanently plugged
into his media


You beyond-gender Guys
who consider the facts
irrelevant


You hypnotized Guys
entranced by all the womanless screens
of misogyny


You slaughtered Guys
who pay for patriarchy's unending Wars
with your very lives

You degendered Guys
whose femininity was gutted
utterly


You unisex Guys
whose restrooms are now sprayed
with semen and urine


You deaf Guys
who cannot hear
any of this


You deconstructed Guys
who don't even know
you exist


You masculine Guys
whose gender is one more natural thing
nearing extinction

You majority Guys
who once were gals
before they were eliminated


You brainwashed Guys
who will deny every word
of this sad treatise


You offended Guys
who are swearing
and refuse to read on


You silenced Guys
who do not really believe women deserve
equality


You tragic Guys—
another endangered
species

# GIRLS

All you unborn Guys
aborted because
you were girls


You baby girl Guys
suffocated and beaten
to death


You unmothered Guys
neglected and rejected
because your mother preferred sons


You unnurtured Guys
who needed but never had
real mothering

You bullied Guys
beaten and molested by your brothers
while parents looked away


Undermined Guys
harassed while your mother chimed
"Boys will be boys"


Mocked Guys
who early learned to play
the stupid fool


You heartbroken Guys
who withdrew as your brother was doted on,
rewarded and feted


You molested Guys
robbed of your maidenhood's first buds
by the family men

Abused Guys
whose innocence and gaiety
were snuffed so soon


You incested Guys
whose very self
was stolen


All you anxious Guys
who grow up fearful of being raped,
kidnapped, murdered, enslaved


You wannabe Guys—
no wonder you don't want
to be women!


You sexless Guys
who would rather be a boy
and stay bosomless

You hunched Guys
who deform your spine
to hide your blossoming breasts


You soccer Guys
who damage your extraordinary brain
to show you can do it too


You glorious Guys
who never give yourselves
enough credit


You lovely young Guys
who can never get
thin enough


All you maddened Guys
who starve your female bodies
and brains

You anorexic Guys
who dread Mother Nature
and your own nature too


You hungry Guys
stuffing and vomiting so no one knows
you want more


You starving Guys
who never stop
eating


You ugly Guys
who work so hard
to get that way


You spooky Guys
who paint your sweet mouths
black

You solitary Guys
who never bond
to anyone


You unloved Guys
whose damaged mothers
could not love you


You modern Guys
who worship your fathers
and denigrate your mothers


You uni-parent Guys
with only one parent
that really counts


You patriarchal Guys
who prefer a godly father
to a lowly mother

You gifted Guys
who do not know your greatest gift
is your femininity


You modest Guys
who bury your brilliance
to fit in


You bookworm Guys
who cannot burrow far enough
away


You shriveled Guys
who always feel ugly under his
cold scrutiny


You unisex Guys
with girlish insides
and a boyish demeanor

You virginal Guys
who kiss a guy
and he responds "holy shit!"


You giggly Guys
who create a sacred space
for girls only


You same-sex Guys
who studiously avoid the sex
that brutalizes


You guarded Guys
whose androgynous faces
hide a secret haven


You gazeless Guys
who dwell
in a cell phone

You hypnotized Guys
who watch TV and eat junk
while Mom works double-time


You dutiful Guys
who raise your siblings
when your parents fail


You innocent Guys
bombarded from every direction
by images of pornography


You overwhelmed Guys
shocked by the ceaseless blare
of man's lust and greed


You confused Guys
who make computer dates
with predators

You sext Guys
who send your body naked
around the world


You unprotected Guys
who will let any boy
maul you


You teen Guys
who allow yourselves to get pregnant
to feel special


You pregnant Guys
with no husband, education,
or prospects


You trusting Guys
who are drugged, stripped
mugged and raped

You gang-raped Guys
whose whole lives are stained by boys
orgasming on hatred


You unseen Guys
overlooked by eyes that are shut
to beauty and grace


You not so pretty Guys
better looking than
most men


You unsung Guys
whose precious beauty passes
unacknowledged and unknown


Oh you beautiful Guys
who are never told
how beautiful you are!

You rare Guys
who are exquisite flowers
in a long dry desert


You lovely Guys
who never know
your own true beauty


You derailed Guys
who have never realized
your divine potential


You gone Guys
who jumped ship
and drowned

# SEXEES

And you hypersexual Guys
who flirt and flash
for attention


You tantalizing Guys
who embody male fantasies
instead of your own


You entranced Guys
with eyes
only for the guys


You captivating Guys
who are really nothing
but captives

You sexy Guys
made for men
only


Insecure Guys
who exhibit your sweet plot of flesh
to everyone


You forever consenting Guys
who do not know it's okay
to say No


Oh you chic Guys
treated like things
rather than beautiful beings


You sad Guys
marketing yourselves on exorbitant stilts
half naked

Careless Guys who give yourselves
to men lacking all respect,
appreciation and understanding


You lusted after Guys
who feel like whores
instead of good women


You flirty Guys
made of needy eyes
and empty skins


You easy Guys
who say yes to any male
who comes sniffing


You sleep-around Guys
who can't say no to anyone
who wants to fuck

Cheap Guys who dress like prostitutes,
always say yes
and do it for free!


You laughing-stock Guys
with eveready boobs and butt
and pussy


You reckless Guys
who numb your pain in fits
of wanton sex


You promiscuous Guys
who just want to party
and forget


You cocksucker Guys
who bow and swallow
nauseating semen

You sex-toy Guys
who have abandoned
all self-respect


You Geisha Guys
whose every gesture is contrived
to entice a customer


You call Guys
beautifully dressed
and sold to the highest bidder


You pricey Guys
soon traded in
for next year's model


You crucified Guys
chopped, cut, hammered
and trashed

You penis-worshipping Guys
who sell yourselves
to the devil


You booty Guys
lifeless
and desperate

# WIVES

You "woman" Guys
which means
"man's wife"


You wifely Guys who create the home,
provide the meals
and service man's other hungers


You betrothed Guys
who mother, lover, shop, clean, cook, garden
assist, nurse and more


You dutiful Guys
taught God created you
to serve your lord and master

You procreative Guys,
eager to have a family
and a few days of glory


You taken for granted Guys
automatically birthing offspring
wanted or not


You trothed Guys,
servant to your lord
and load


You necessary Guys
who must provide his planet
with more and more sons


You super-slave Guys
purchased for sex
and heirs

Modern Guys who do not know
how to hold a baby
since the mothers never showed you


Unmotherly Guys who shake
and hyper-stimulate your infants
and know no peace


You contemporary Guys
who ignore your child's needs
while seeking your own fulfillment


You patriarchal Guys
whose name records father and husband
and erases the mothers who bore and raised them


You quasi-liberated Guys
who shoulder two male lineages
with a hyphen

You nameless Guys
called Mrs. Tom,
Dick or Harry


You undetectable Guys
who stand invisible
behind your man


You wedded Guys
who follow him
wherever he goes


You conjugal Guys
who pace from room to room
behind the curtains


You pathetic Guys
beaten and raped whenever
your spouse desires

You pariah Guys
hidden from
the light of day


You gated Guys
confined by walls
and millions of obscuring veils


You inscrutable Guys
hidden behind masks
divised by male surgeons


You disabled Guys
who do not dare to drive
but must be driven by a man


You dependent Guys
who must ask for permission
to spend his money

You Guys forever in-danger
who must be scrupulously
guarded


You polygamy Guys
added to his harem
to improve his service and might


You chattel Guys
whose husbands own various spouses
while you get one


You regressive Guys
who ran from freedom to marry
the worst oppression


You redundant Guys
whose mates stock extra lovers,
wives and children

You devoted Guys
who neglect your own children
to satisfy your man


You imprisoned Guys
who pass your days cleaning
and gossiping


You complacent Guys
habituated to the daily
prison drill


You closeted Guys
who limp along useless
and fade away


You phobic Guys
who stay home
your whole lives

You wed-locked Guys
occasionally let out on parole
with the girls


You fortressed Guys
who chauffeur and shop
in menacing vans


Appended Guys
terrified
to be independent


You cell-phone Guys
panicked by a moment
alone


You housebound Guys
who fear to go out
into his world

You lonely Guys
caught in a bubble until he leaves
and it bursts


You widowed Guys
whose lives are meaningless
without a man


You "behind every man" Guys
who sacrificed your calling
so he could live his


You good cook Guys
whose satisfying meals
made Michelin star chefs of your sons


You downtrodden Guys
crushed by children,
career and a needy husband

Subjugated Guys
who pay with your lives
and do not know it


You selfless Guys
who give and give and give
yourselves away

▽

# PATRIARCHEES

You billion fold Guys
constantly meditating
on Men


You male-identified Guys
who are the protectors
of male privilege


You duped Guys
raised to believe that Men
are superior to Women


You biased Guys
whose mothers were powerless
while your fathers were treated like gods

You adaptor Guys
for whom his phallus
is the only bridge to validity


Oh you subservient Guys
with man at the top
and woman always at the bottom.


You adjusted Guys
who do not mind playing
second fiddle


You safe Guys
who need a male bodyguard
ever beside you


You sugar-sweet Guys
whose voices can barely
be heard

You faux Guys
babbling baby-talk
in falsetto voices


You choir Guys
who are the joyful holiday voice
of male-dominant religion


You melodious Guys
the patriarchs tried to imitate
by castrating little boys


You sublime Guys
who will only sing the names
of male gods


You believer Guys
who see God as a guy
seated on a throne in the sky

You clever Guys
who keep your intelligence,
talents and wisdom hidden

You deferential Guys
whose eyes and expectations lower
before the dominant sex

You protective Guys
who protect only the well being
of men

You cheerleader Guys
who cheer only
for the opposite sex

You adoring Guys
with eyes
only for your guy

You transparent Guys
so pretty, thin
and unassuming


You voiceless Guys
who always let your guy answer
for you


You suffocating Guys
whose voices are silenced
by diamond chokers


You insecure Guys
always encircled
by domineering males


You leeched Guys
whose beauty is drained
moment by moment

You obsequious Guys
who hang on man's every word
and gesture


You doggy Guys
who fetch, fawn, guard
and even do tricks


You apologetic Guys
who always aim
to please


You ladylike Guys
who never stop trying
to be perfect


You needy Guys
who need men to like you
since you do not like yourselves

You married Guys
who give your energy to your husband
denying your children


You ask-nothing Guys
who compromise with unspeakable vulgarity
constantly


You slavish Guys
put down and controlled
by men


You long-suffering Guys
who put up with put-downs
day in, day out


You sorry Guys
always apologizing
for everything

You doormat Guys
who dream that one day he will love you
if you only do what he wants


You obedient Guys
told what to buy,
what to wear, what to eat and think


You objectified Guys
who work all day
on your appearance


You make-over Guys
made over and over for men
who are considered satisfactory as they are


You vain Guys
whose vapid pride will never compare
to the fossilized pride of males

You skinny Guys
whose food is monitored
by beefy bulky over-fed males


You taut Guys
wound up like walky-talky dolls
for his pleasure


You creative Guys
dancing as fast as you can
to his tune


You revolutionary Guys
who join men in changing the world
by destroying


You puppet Guys
who perform to perfection
his script and his score

You robotic Guys
who became machines
in your crazy effort to please


You miniature Guys
who shrank
into shiny trophies


You little Guys
who became something,
not somebody


You sycophantic Guys
petrified
to be yourselves


You stunted Guys
who could never grow up
under his sheltering wing

You ornamental Guys
potted, pruned
and fruitless


You made up Guys
so lovely to look at
who never live


You unaspiring Guys
who sport Harvard tee-shirts
instead of going to Harvard


You giggling Guys
who laugh it all
off


You confused Guys
who have no idea what you want
since nobody ever asked you

You postponed Guys
always waiting for some man to come back
from work or war or who knows where


You unsuccessful Guys
who never achieve success because
you don't aim for it


You shallow Guys
with no sense of your own depth
or worth


You lazy Guys
who want men to run the world
no matter what the cost


You compliant Guys
who obey all
his Taboos

You deferential Guys
who honor the great Silence
on Male Violence


You simple Guys
who think men are programmed by God
or genes to be tyrants


You cynical Guys
who imagine Mother Nature created man
to conquer


You submissive Guys
convinced that Nature
made man brutal


You manipulated Guys
who were taught that men are naturally violent
and who bought it

You unconscious Guys
who think that testosteromania
is natural


You masochistic Guys
who embrace male domination
and destruction of life


You battered Guys
who let men yell, insult
and strike both you and the earth


You pathetic Guys
led by men like lambs
to the slaughter


You conditioned Guys
who submit to mental and physical
torture

You automaton Guys
who even let your partners rape
your daughters


You hollow Guys
whose life-giving essence
has been drained


You derivative Guys
who dream you were constructed
from some guy's rib


You patriarchalized Guys
who can no longer hear
Mother Nature


You willful Guys
whose wombs say No
and at your peril you defy them

You stubborn Guys
who force your bodies to birth lives
they cannot conceive or carry


You ever pregnant Guys
who spread a human plague
upon the world


You spoiled Guys
who turn away from your responsibility
and power


You blindered Guys
who cannot imagine equality
and will not try


You invalid Guys
who require a man
for validation

You voided Guys
with stars in your eyes
only for guys


You co-opted Guys
content to vote
for men only


You treacherous Guys
who sacrifice a rising mountain of daughters
on patriarchy's altar


You political Guys
who sing the chorus
of male domination


You Muse Guys
who amuse male artists
with endless inspiration

You "behind every man" Guys
who abandon your calling
to steer a man to glory


You wedded Guys
who keep on picking up
his dirty underwear


You Guys
who can only find God
in a man


You poker-faced Guys
who pretend you don't notice
that your sex is rarely represented


You charmer Guys
who tactfully overlook all the inequalities
hoping to get your way

You self-denying Guys
who let your talents
go to seed


You denier Guys
who tell yourselves
misogyny is rare


You make-believe Guys
who pretend
you are free


You supporting Guys
in a minor role where your actions
seldom matter


You laboring Guys
whose souls expire
in toxic barren offices

You extra Guys
with no real role in his zillion dollar
multimedia production


You token Guys
rarely president, chief or priest
no matter how you excel


You overlooked Guys
never up for consideration
or even in the running


You displaced Guys
replaced by the next wife
or assistant


You patriotic Guys
whose country belongs
to an unruly mob of men

You taxed Guys
who pay for his uncontrollable violence,
prisons, weapons and wars


You exhausted Guys
who keep dragging woman's mountainous burden
on your aching backs


You trapped Guys
who slave night and day for your pimp
unable to flee


You frightened Guys
who stumble onward in denial
and shame


You devastated Guys
whose childish hearts adored a patriarch
and were crushed

You duped Guys
who fell for it
hook, line and sinker


You helpless Guys
who are totally afraid
to take charge


You useless Guys
who are numbed by pills
and booze


You ruined Guys
in ruins like the rest of the world
thanks to power-hungry men


You cowardly Guys
with no desire whatsoever
to change

You stony Guys
silent before mankind's monstrous
War on Nature


You defeated Guys
missing in the losing proposition
that is patriarchy


You gutless Guys
afraid to be free, to be courageous,
to take a chance


You disempowered Guys
afraid, afraid, afraid
to reveal yourselves


You disappeared Guys
whose absence dooms
the world

You abdicated Guys
where
are you?

▽

# WOMAN HATERS

All you patriarchal Guys
who idolize men
and look down on women


You unhappy Guys
who dislike yourself
and therefore all of womankind


You post-mother Guys
who preferred your father
to your mother


You biased Guys
whose mothers were disempowered
and fathers elevated to kings

You patriarchalized Guys
who view mothers as dwarfs
and fathers as giants


You assistant Guys
who call female clients Honey
and male clients Sir


You ordinary Guys
who generously critique women
and spare the men.


You loyal Guys
who ridicule feminists,
too afraid to admit you agree


You jealous Guys who sabotage
even your daughter's
opportunities and achievements.

You envious Guys
who can't stand a courageous woman
surpassing you.


You imperialized Guys
who have adopted male brutality
and scapegoat women


You obedient Guys
who support your master
by putting rebellious women down


You brainwashed Guys
who cut the genitals
out of virgins


You snarling Guys
who tote kids and guns
and revile the women who run free

You bulldog Guys
bred and trained to attack any woman
who dares to stand up


Vicious Guys who attack
females young and old
because patriarchy sanctions it


Aggressive Guys
who insult your mothers and children
for emotional release


And you pious Guys
who ruthlessly keep women
out of the pulpit


You defector Guys
who identify with the aggressor
and turn against your own kind

You starlet Guys
who became wealthy from making movies
about the destruction of women


You Madam Guys
who sell traumatized runaway girls
to anyone


You perverted Guys
who help your man rape girls,
enslave and murder


You cold-blooded Guys
who simply don't care about
your sisters' welfare


You colluding guys
who have fallen in love
with your jailer

You fraternal Guys
who have joined in the abhorrence
of womanhood


You self-hating Guys
who hate your female body and mind
as much as men do


You sheepish Guys
who stampede with the guys
toward certain disaster

▽

# SELF DEFORMERS

And you stagey Guys
painstakingly
masked


You made-up Guys
who keep your unwelcome face
undercover with paint


You baked Guys
bronzed to seem more attractive—
as if you weren't already


All you high heeled Guys
who hobble
in pain

Spiked Guys
who destroy your feet
to gain some stature


You stigmatized Guys
who pierce, tattoo, inject, implant
your living body


Skin-deep Guys
who trash the magical face
Mother Earth gave you


You tragic Guys
who choose a man-made mask
over Mother Nature's loving design


You disappeared Guys
snipped and stitched into his
latest facial construct

You surgeried Guys
who no longer bear any resemblance
to yourselves


You never good-enough Guys
who make men rich inflating women's breasts
with deadly toxin


You grotesque Guys
who risk your health to rouse overgrown babies
with your oversized tits


You depressed Guys
damaged by diets, drugs and surgeries
for men who cannot love


You deformed Guys
who cut up your body
for men who do not even respect you

You self-mutilating Guys
who bite on giant tits
of rage


You hysterical Guys
who waste your force
in an endless river of screams


You obese Guys
who turn your back on life
to simply eat


Oh you empty Guys
who never stop filling up
with food


You addicted Guys
who destroy your lives
with devastating drugs

You disembodied Guys
who must cut your limbs
to feel alive


You faceless Guys
whose natural countenance you traded
for wrinkle-free


You genocidal Guys
who slowly starve your bodies
to death


You hyper-sensitive Guys
who were manufactured
for anxiety


You countless Guys
scarcely mothered,
starved for a mother's love

All you self-loathing Guys
who are tossed about on turbulent waves
of worthlessness

▽

# MEN-WOMEN

You wannabe Guys
who never liked or wanted to be
female


You done Guys
who refuse to be
mere women


You shorn Guys
who chop off your hair
to look like a man


You Guys
who parody his ugliness
with butch cuts, black leather and chains

You Guys in pants all over the world
who copy the uniform
of the rulers


You occupied Guys
who aim to be great men
not true women


You expropriated Guys
who are efficient cogs
in the machine of Patriarchy


You buddy Guys
who forgot how to be sisterly—
whatever that means


You heady Guys
astray in the maze of masculine
confusion and stupidity

You compliant Guys
who measure yourselves
by male standards


You scalped Guys
euphoric to get into his show
at any price


You coarse Guys
who banished refinement
to become as crude as a man


You soldier Guys
who throw away your lives
for the fatherland


You terrorist Guys
in love with men
in love with death

You armored Guys
who cover up the woman inside
so men will include you


You body-building Guys
who model yourselves
on hypertrophied masculinity


You masculine Guys
who had to become men
in order to participate


You hardened Guys
so tough no man can hurt you
anymore


You competitive Guys
who can defeat
any man

You boastful Guys
who have succeeded in becoming lazy,
smug and sullen as many men


You daredevil Guys
who show as much disregard for Life
as he does


You alienated guys
who no longer know how to listen
to Mother Nature


You unmaternal Guys
whose unloved mothers couldn't bond
so now you can't either


You brusque Guys
who adopted his ways
and became heartless machines

You decadent Guys
who emulate
his greed


You loveless Guys
who transform your rage
into icy seductions


You man-eating Guys
who graze on phalluses
rising and falling


You ruined Guys
who go from lust to lust
and fuck to fuck


You mannish Guys
who long to be men
and practically succeed

You one-of-the Guys
who get all your esteem
from guys


You turncoat Guys
who imbibe male hormones
to purge yourself of the feminine


You crossover Guys
who forfeit your goddess nature
to enter maledom


You imitation Guys
manufactured in the image
of patriarchy


You switched Guys
whose breasts were sliced,
vaginas shut, rods attached

You default Guys
who succumbed
to universal Brotherhood


You demented Guys
who threw away your birthright,
wishing to be a man


You modern Guys
who never learned that Motherhood
is the supreme profession


You self-centered Guys
who want to have children yet be free
of your great responsibility


You selfish Guys
who damage your innocent offspring
with your needy narcissism

You driven Guys
who stunt your children's growth
by your absence


You ripped-off Guys
who traded in your womanhood
for a scrap of power


You sorrowful Guys
who handed over your soul
for a longer leash


You wasted Guys
who abandoned our responsibility
to care for Life


You on-call Guys
who stand at attention
hearkening to the call "You Guys"

You eliminated Guys
born female,
in training to be little men


You Guys
who chose to be a fake man
instead of a real woman


You faux Guys
trying to be men,
who never will be


You confused Guys
who must learn to rise up as women
not imitation men


▽

# REBELS

You offended Guys
who hate being called a guy
when you aren't one


You soft-spoken Guys
who purr like
lion cubs


You squealy Guys
who saturate the atmosphere
with feminine energy


You incessantly talkative Guys
starved
for ears that hear

You intrusive Guys
whose restless heels click click click
across the world


You towering Guys
tottering in stilettos
to force men to take notice


You ferocious Guys
who will not tolerate being
his underdog


You draconian Guys
puffing dark smoke
from your nostrils


You dolly Guys
sexed up in an act of aggression
against men

You manic Guys
who spend all his money in a tantrum
of spending


You exhibitionistic Guys
who force men to see you,
shamelessly female


You defiant Guys
proud of your coal black lips
and nails like bloody stigmata


You punk Guys
who satirize patriarchy's love of death
with skulls, spikes and chains


You apocalyptic Guys
who groove on prophesying
the world's destruction

You cancerous Guys
whose very cells rise up
and multiply in wrathful rebellion


You allergic Guys
whose bodies explode,
I am poisoned !


You hysterical Guys
bursting
with blood curdling screams


You ironic Guys
keenly aware
that men rarely do their share


You ill-tempered Guys
who never stop chewing
on hostile thoughts

You hostile Guys
who can't get over
your bottomless resentment


You resentful Guys
obsessed with male privilege,
arrogance and incompetence


You insolent Guys
who bathe men in looks
of acid loathing


You histrionic Guys
who parade your victimhood
with gusto


You single Guys
who form a threatening army
of defectors

You striker Guys
who firmly withhold
your womanly services


You divorced Guys
who will not take it
anymore


You renegade Guys
who refuse to be
his woman


You brassy Guys
toughened by moms who struggled
for every crumb


You tough Guys
who had to fight and fight for the right
to play the game

You sharp Guys
who keep on fighting
to stay in the game


You strident Guys
whose sentences and gestures
are edged in steel


You pushy Guys
who bulldoze everything
in your way


You shrill Guys
who bristle, boast
and bite


You determined Guys
who are edgy, pushy,
competitive and vindictive

You good-as Guys
who are promiscuous, assaultive,
wild and deadly


You arrogant Guys
who can out-dominate the guys
and are just as scary


You avenger Guys
who gobble up one man
after the next


You death-row Guys
who killed your deadly husband
before he killed you


You protesting Guys
who never stop
protesting

# OUTSIDERS

You outsider Guys
eternally waiting for the Queen's gate
to swing open


All you dazed Guys
who sleepwalk through life
in a dream


You phantom Guys
haunting the halls of patriarchal science,
commerce and government


Bored silly Guys
not even interested enough
to notice men

Resigned Guys
convinced men have destroyed the planet
so why even discuss it


You fed-up Guys
who no longer listen
to anything know-it-all men have to say


All you storytelling Guys
whose sons became
the famous authors


You out-of-place Guys
who feel strange being called a guy
when you are a gal


You chronically ill Guys
who cannot cope
with his world

Turned-off Guys
deafened by constant blasts
of violent noise, talk, sports and war


You downcast Guys
who take lifelong refuge
in therapy offices


You perceptive Guys
with no significant part in the play
who no longer want one


You clear-sighted Guys
who can see through
it all


And you blindered Guys
who black out
the continual threats

You outsider Guys
who do not accept the delusion of patriarchy
and never will


You opt-out Guys
who opted out
of the gender mess men made


You remote Guys
who reside in faraway realms
where men cannot reach you


You drop-out Guys,
non-voters, non-graduates,
who gave up on his world


You untouchable Guys
buried under
innumerable burqas

You New Age Guys
who levitate from your bodies
to escape reality


You blank Guys
who block
even your own thoughts


You self-doubting Guys
with a fraction of the confidence
of most men


You censored Guys,
distorted, berated and deleted
from male media


You verbally gifted Guys
who created language
now controlled by men

You vague Guys
clueless of the genius
of the integrated female brain


Impoverished Guys
who heal with living plants,
whose grandsons are wealthy doctors


You ignorant Guys
still unaware of the Great Mother's
long silenced civilization


Doomed Guys
for whom your own history,
tradition and wisdom are long forgotten


You lonely Guys
who are exiles in the country
of your birth

You pathologized Guys
whose incurable disease
is Womanhood


You denigrated Guys
completely convinced
you are trash


You alien Guys
born female
in dominator patriarchy


You mothery Guys
who have no authority in the eyes
of his society


You conquered Guys
who possess not a hundredth of the planet
men have stolen

You powerless Guys
who have almost no say or status
anywhere in this world


You nobody Guys
sure you are
"Nobody too"


You long forgotten Guys
who barely know
you exist


You disempowered Guys
afraid, afraid
to reveal yourselves


You muted Guys
too terrified
to speak up

You paralyzed Guys
who dare not look
into the abyss of your fears


You frozen Guys
who are unable to do
what you want and should do


You displaced Guys
who cannot find yourselves
anywhere, even here


You resigned Guys
who will hate this raging righteous hymn,
this requiem


You Guys in flight
who keep running
and weeping

Rootless Guys
who have no place
of your own


You diminished Guys
who have never known your own
vast pure strength


You suicide Guys
whose feelings of worthlessness
won the day


You disappeared Guys
whose absence dooms
the world


You abdicated Guys
where
are you?

# SURVIVORS

You worn down Guys
who struggle every day
to keep your head and your spirit up


You heroic Guys
who have survived untold harassment
by patriarchal society


You working Guys
unable to say what you think
of men's behavior


You supermom Guys
who think you can do everything
even if you can't

You author Guys
who know you won't get published
if you say what you know


You grassroot Guys
who know nothing good
can flourish under male domination


You single Guys
who work, tend the house
and raise the children


You martyred Guys
who struggle to accomplish
the impossible


You independent Guys
who keep trying
and trying

You sleeping beauty Guys
waking from a curse
of millennia

▽

# VICTIMS ALL

Oh you female Guys
who are victims, victims,
victims all

You illiterate Guys
deprived of education
who cannot read this or any poem

You tented Guys
who watch life go by
through the bars of your cage

You legislated Guys
whose bodies are controlled
by male politicians and police

You licensed Guys
whose movements are as restricted
as the animals and the rivers


You irrelevant Guys
whose ideas are endlessly
invalidated


You mom-in-law Guys
who are the butt of jokes,
scorn and ridicule


You homemaker Guys whose sons take
your best recipes minus the love
and are proclaimed Chefs


You ambitious Guys
whose strivings will never
be realized

You masterful Guys
who have no authority
in patriarchy


You accomplished Guys
who would be three times as successful
if you were men


You secondary Guys
who always come second,
even on gravestones


You cornucopian Guys
who provide half the food
and own not a hundredth of the land


You oppressed Guys
forever overlooked
because you are not a man

You decapitated Guys
whose thoughts are
systematically axed


You first-lady Guys
demeaned by his news,
tabloids and pornography


You professional Guys
whose colleagues and employees slight you
as girls


You operatic Guys
whose heavenly arias are always hacked
by coughing boors


You ripped-off Guys
whose sons trade dishes made with love
for money and fame

You brilliant Guys
whose ideas are continually
stolen


You vulnerable and caring Guys
whose hearts were open
and broken


You bereft Guys
whose irreplaceable sons were killed
in patriarchy's never-ending War


You Guys who were dumped
after decades of homemaking,
cooking, love-making and child-rearing


You reified Guys
who were used and abused
until you became useless burdens

You candidate Guys
lynched by macho media
and their flunkies—or shot dead


You caretaker Guys
assaulted by the male patients
in your care


You abused Guys
bossed and exploited
even by the sons you birthed


You neurotic Guys
who over-run counselors' offices
unable to cope


You sunk Guys
whose strength is sapped,
who cannot pull yourselves up

You masseuse Guys
who service men
with orgasms


You desperate Guys
who sell your body to anyone for sex
to support your families


You prostituted Guys
sexually exploited as children
and forever after


You comfort Guys
forced to provide soldiers
with sexual pleasure


You sex-worker Guys
beaten by pimps, fucked by perverts
and jailed by the police

You trashed Guys
raped or unprotected
and now infected


You assaulted Guys
raped in the military, at parties, in your own bed
from birth to death


You terrorized Guys
whose lives are forever
in danger


You Guys who are
the victims
of gendercide


Insulted Guys
put down every day
and afraid to stop it

Unhealthy Guys
malnourished by fake foods
devised by men


Denatured Guys
sickened by the electromagnetic machines
men prefer to Life


You polluted Guys
whose bodies are constantly damaged
by his waves, chemicals and rays


You sick Guys
made allergic, cancerous, degenerate, infertile
by man's never-ending pollutions


You toxic Guys
who poison your babies
with your poisoned breast milk

All you infertile Guys
who birth unformed fetuses,
miscarry and cannot conceive


You sick-to-death Guys
sterilized by patriarchy's
zillion poisons


You crucified Guys
whose every body part
has been mutilated by men


You acid-burned Guys
whose hopeful lives were dead-ended
by sub-humans


You mutilated Guys
pierced, pricked, tattooed, incised,
injected and castrated

You dismembered Guys
whose faces, breasts, clitorises, labia, bellies
and wombs were excoriated


You missing Guys
murdered and dismembered
by husbands, lovers, brothers and strangers


You murdered Guys
who usually die
at the hands of your own family


You casualty Guys
killed by soldiers,
three-quarters of every war's dead


You inconsequential Guys
blown up by bombs more often
than soldiers

You woman-shield Guys
sacrificed to protect
criminals


You prime minister Guys
who are usually
assassinated


Ah you endlessly hated Guys
assassinated by men every hour of every day
on every continent


You tormented Guys
harassed, mugged, drugged, raped, battered, beaten,
strangled, suffocated and stoned


You taboo Guys
whose sacred image is gouged,
pulverized and incinerated by male marauders

You dead Guys
slaughtered with countless millions
of your gender


You reincarnated Guys
who remember hanging from a tree
or burning on a stake—one of the millions


You Goddess worshiping Guys
attacked by Muslim,
Christian, Jew alike


You sphinx Guys
who for millennia have born
the monumental burden of his jealousy


All you Guys
who are the minute-by-minute victims
of male supremacy

You voiceless Guys
who live your whole life
without saying what you really feel


You icy Guys
silent as prehistoric glaciers
just beginning to melt


You disoriented Guys
waking from a five-thousand-year nightmare
of slavery


You unknown Guys
unheard for hundreds and thousands
and millions of nows


You patient Guys
who will someday-over-the-rainbow
have what is yours

You back-up Guys
who will have to rebuild the world
he is destroying


You wizened Guys
whose wisdom still goes
unheeded


You other Guys
who are outsiders no matter
what you do


You woman Guys
whose name has been deleted
from human history


You throw-away Guys
who constitute more than half
of the human population

You anguished Guys
who must watch your sisters being crushed
again and again


You tragic Guys
damaged, damaged, damaged
by millennia of abuse


You heart-broken heart-breaking Guys
we miss and mourn and grieve
like hell


You tortured Guys
battered, bullied, castrated, chained, enslaved,
incarcerated, incested, incinerated


You kidnapped, mocked, molested, mutilated,
poisoned, porned, prostituted, raped,
slashed, stalked and slaughtered

You mocked for-millennia Guys who were
actresses, babes, bags, ball-busters, barbies,
biddies, bitches, call girls, chicks and cocksuckers

concubines, cows, dames,
dolls, dykes, feminazis,
foxes, hags, harlots, hens and kittens

You man-hating Guys,
minxes, prick-teases, prostitutes, prudes,
pussies, sassy-pants, sex-pots, sluts and spinsters

You undermined.
puffed and pounded,
nailed and drilled

You deconstructed Guys,
you forgotten Guys,
you entranced Guys

consenting, apologetic, undignified,
captive and erased,
one with the Guys


Oh you sleepers, zombies,
mummies, ghosts and slaves,
wake and arise before it is too late


You ephemeral Guys
who just like the real guys
will soon be gone


You juicy tarts and tomboys,
vixens, whores
and witches


You stray Guys
who will some day return
to your own wise womanly heart

You prodigal Guys
whose homecoming the Earth
will one day greet with shouts of joy


You cocooned Guys
who will one day break out
and spread your dazzling rainbow wings


You matter Guys,
what happens to you
happens to all of Creation

▽

# VICTORS

You irrepressible Guys
who keep on being women
no matter what


You double X Guys
who carry the chromosome that does not
decay but repairs


You strong Guys
who know how to survive
under any condition


You transitional Guys
who survive and even thrive
in this chaos

You breakaway Guys
who gather in cafes and living rooms
conspiring with other women


You uppity Guys
slandered and shunned
who keep on speaking and creating


You androgynous Guys
who became the guy
you wanted to marry


You successful Guys
who must live with the envy
of gals still chained


You warrior Guys
who keep on, keep on fighting
and never give up

You cutting-edge Guys
who chop paths through the jungle
for the people of the future


You courageous Guys
who risk your very lives
to speak the truth


You unstoppable Guys
who flow round and over and under
every obstacle


You mated Guys
who can fly with a man like a bird
balancing your conjoined wings


You amazing double-winged Guys
who can soar
over it all

You life-giving Guys
who keep renewing the natural world,
ever under attack


You maternal Guys
who bleed, conceive and gestate Life
in your ever hopeful, renewing wombs


You superhuman Guys
who give birth
to everyone on earth


You tender Guys
who mother the plants,
the animals and the people


You indestructible Guys
who gather and harvest,
manufacture, manage and guide

You earthy Guys
who grow and cook the food
that feeds and heals the human family


You giving Guys
who sacrifice your lives
to raise a healthy humanity


You enduring Guys
who walk endless miles
to keep your children fed and alive


You nurturing Guys
who hug the lonely, feed the hungry,
heal the sick


You caring Guys
who birth and nurse, comfort and encourage
Earth's children

You motherly Guys
who greet each new life with smiles
that glow with love


You loving Guys
whose warming embrace
means everything


You reliable Guys
who carry the world on your heads
and hips and in your wombs


You nevertheless Guys
who continue and survive and overcome
and triumph


You matrix Guys
who hold this amazing
vibrating web together

You miraculously graceful Guys
who dance through the hell realms
of patriarchy


You white-haired, grandmotherly Guys
who patiently guide us
with your slow sure care


You cultivated Guys
who are culture itself—
who create it and pass it on


You indigenous Guys
who still carry on humanity's
oldest wisdom traditions


You yogini Guys
who take to the woods
to live simply, truly and harmlessly

You nun Guys
who in your solitude
conserve the last vestiges of the feminine


You contemplative Guys
ever praying to lessen the agony
of this world


You generous Guys
centered in the Source
continuously bubbling up and spilling over


You anonymous Guys
who generate cornucopias
of inspiring Art


You visionary Guys
who can see everything
and share it

You salty Guys
who spice each moment
with quick warm laughs


You funny Guys
whose laughter rocks
the hollow halls of his-story


You refined Guys
dancing and singing and praying
amid all this violent cacophony


You celebratory Guys
thankful to be a little freer
than your grandmothers


You brightly shining Guys
who uplift all Creation
with your dazzling beauty

You lovely Guys
who are fresh
rare flowers


You gorgeous Guys
who are shimmering fountains
of divine grace


You humble Guys
who simply serve and serve
and serve


You modest Guys
who are the last true hope
of the world


You saintly Guys
who give everything you have
and ask nothing in return

You brave Guys
whose voices quake and thunder
through the terrible terror


You holy Guys
who calmly endure
all the pain


You transcendent Guys
able to rise
above this trying incarnation


You martyred Guys
who shed your lives
in the searing flames


You phoenix Guys
who lay your eggs
in everywoman's ashes

You indomitable Guys
who keep time on Creation's drum
with your own bodies


You virtuous Guys
who are Love's
very embodiment


You bodhisattva Guys
come to heal the world
with your tenderness and kindness


You prayerful Guys
who offer your love and light
to the world


You brilliant Guys
who flood the whole universe
with miraculous love

You loving Guys
more beautiful even
than God


You effulgent Guys
who radiate
a piercing pure light


You victorious Guys
manifest in a myriad forms
since time immemorial

Oh you glorious Guys
who were amazons, anonymous, aunties, courtesans and crones,
daughters, empresses, feminists, gals, girls, goddesses,
godmothers, grandmothers, homemakers, housekeepers,
ladies, maidens, maids, misses, mistresses, mothers,
mothers of God, nuns, poetesses, priestesses,
queens, secretaries, sisters, sphinxes,
suffragettes, virgins, wives
and women

before you
became
Guys

▽

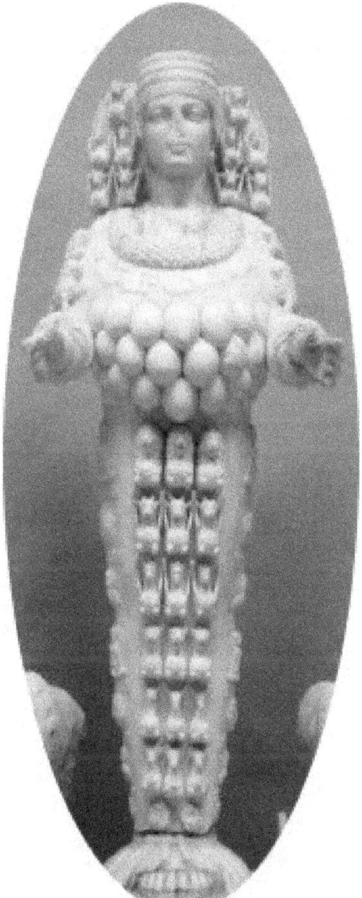

## ACKNOWLEDGMENTS

THANKS to the amazing friends who sustained me with their energy and love during the years of creating this work: Barbara Brooker, Carol Fabric, Angelika Gates, Linda Johnsen, Patricia Laferriere, Nancy Leatzow—and the tireless feminists Maya Angelou, Gloria Steinem and their dear ally Hillary Clinton.

JANINE CANAN, graduate of Stanford University with distinction and NYU School of Medicine, is a psychiatrist as well as the author of twenty-some books—most recently *Love Is My Religion*, a three volume compilation of the teachings of Mata Amritanandamayi, and *Consciousness*, a new collection of poetry. Janine's work has been honored with an NEA publication grant for *Of Your Seed*, the Koppelman Award for *She Rises like the Sun: Invocations of the Goddess* by *Contemporary American Women Poets*, *Health and Spirituality's* Best Book Award for *Messages from Amma: In the Language of the Heart,* and the Sacred Feminine Award. Visit JanineCanan.com to learn more.

*Goddesses, Goddesses*
"Canan's two great loves—of language and of life—are poured onto every page for our pleasure and inspiration."
—Mara Keller, director, Women's Spirituality, California Institute of Integral Studies

*Ardor*
"Astonishing poetry, very pure. A book you keep by your side like a bible."
—Barbara Brooker, author of Love, Sometimes